T0196278

FROM
A Woman's
POINT OF VIEW

FROM
A Woman's
POINT OF VIEW

Mz. Yvette D

authorHOUSE®

AuthorHouse™
1663 Liberty Drive
Bloomington, IN 47403
www.authorhouse.com
Phone: 1-800-839-8640

First published by AuthorHouse   01/04/2012

ISBN: 978-1-4685-3094-0 (sc)
ISBN: 978-1-4685-3093-3 (ebk)

Library of Congress Control Number: 2011963107

Printed in the United States of America

Contents

Introduction vii

Chapter 1   I Know What I Want....................................1

Chapter 2   Could This Be It?..5

Chapter 3   Reality Check... 11

Chapter 4   The Big Break... 15

Chapter 5   Just Another Secret................................. 21

Chapter 6   Finally, I Can Live..................................... 27

Chapter 7   Woman To Woman................................. 33

Chapter 8   Strictly Platonic.. 39

Chapter 9   It's All Over, Or Is It?................................ 43

Chapter 10 When Sunday Comes 47

Chapter 11 When You Least Expect It 51

Conclusion   63

Contact Information 67

Introduction

*I*t's Destiny's normal routine for a Sunday morning. The alarm clock goes off at 7:00 a.m. She hears the extremely loud beeping over and over and over, which seemed like it had been sounding for hours. She slowly turns over and hits the snooze button, wanting her usual extra 10 minutes of sleep. Along comes Ciara, her beautiful, bright-eyed 10 year old daughter. Ciara could hear the alarm across the hall in her bedroom. "Get up momma, it's time for church!," shouts Ciara, as she sits and bounces on the bed next to her mother, smiling as if she'd just received the greatest gift in the world. Destiny sits up in the bed, gives a great big stretch, and tells Ciara how important it is for momma to get her extra 10 minutes of sleep. She tells her how the extra sleep time helps momma to not have baggy eyes and how it keeps her from being tired and cranky during the rest of the day. Knowing she was only making this up, Ciara listened patiently to her mom. Ciara tells Destiny now she knows why her mom is so beautiful, it's from all the times she hit the button when the alarm went off in the mornings. They laughed and hugged each other; lots of smiles and giggles from the two of them. The alarm goes off again which tells Ciara it's time for her to get dressed for church. She already knew what she wanted to wear. She had chosen a beautiful white dress with a gorgeous yellow satin bow. She decided to wear her yellow socks, trimmed with delicate white lace, which matched the bow on the dress perfectly. Ciara chose to wear her white shoes with a small gold buckle to compliment the outfit. As she's leaving the room, she yells to her dad, "good morning pop!" He replied, "good morning baby girl!" Destiny gives another big stretch before getting out of bed to begin her day; thinking, how did she get to this place in her life? How did her life become so wonderful, compared to how it had been the past few years? After all she had been through, she finds herself in a beautiful home, with a wonderful husband, and the sweetest child in the world. This is Destiny's story—from a woman's point of view.

Chapter 1

~ I Know What I Want ~

*L*ife can dish out some very bitter pills that we must swallow in order to grow and move forward. We may never know or understand <u>all</u> the things we encounter in life, but we must know that it all works together for our good—even though it may not look like it at the time.

You see, Destiny has been hurt by so many people. She's been abandoned, misunderstood and abused. Destiny grew up in Southern Mississippi. She was raised by her aunt after her parents were killed in a car accident when she was 10 years old. Needless to say, she's had to deal with some of the more important times of her life without having a mother or father. Her parents weren't there for her first date, her prom, or her high school graduation. She never had those much needed one-on-one conversations with her mom about boys and relationships; or those conversations that would teach her about life in general. Her mom never had the opportunity to teach Destiny how to make the family's secret spaghetti sauce or how to make her famous choco choco brownies.

Although she vaguely remembered some of the times she shared with her parents, especially her mom, this was a time in her life that she needed them more than ever. Destiny thought back, remembering when she was about 7 years old. Her parents took her to this huge shopping mall. She saw what she considered to be the most beautiful painting she had ever seen. It wasn't so much the beauty of the painting, as it was the picture that was painted. It was a picture of a family; a mother, a father, and a beautiful baby. They were standing in front of a huge house closed in by a stunning white fence. From that moment, Destiny realized what she wanted. She wanted a family like that! She would one day grow up and have her very own.

Because her parents died when she was such a young age, Destiny never really felt secure. She felt abandoned, lonely, and unsure of her future. Although brought up in church, the direction for her life was so unclear. Her aunt did a great job raising her, but there's nothing like being raised by your parents.

Not long after moving in with her aunt, Destiny was sexually abused while on her way to the corner store. She joyfully walked and sang as if she didn't have a care in the world. A man she had seen in the neighborhood many times was walking towards her. Still singing and tossing her coin bag from one hand to the other, Destiny began to feel a little scared and uneasy. The man was getting closer to her, but was not trying to move so she could pass. He grabbed her and put his hand over her mouth. She was so scared; too scared to scream, too scared to really breathe. He pushed her into an abandoned shed a few feet from the sidewalk. He began to tell her he's been watching her and he really liked her. He touched her in places she was taught to be private. He began kissing her cheeks and rubbing all over her little body. He told her to never tell anyone or he would do it again and again. Of course, Destiny was terrified. She continued on to the store wiping her eyes and making sure her clothes were properly fixed. The man walked away saying, "remember, don't tell, or I'll get you again." She returned home and never told a soul what had happened. This was a lot for a 10 year old to handle; first losing her parents in a fatal car accident, then being molested. She was really scared, hurt, and confused by all of this, but never shared it with anyone. Still to this day, it's been her little secret. It was something that she didn't think of anymore, as if it never happened. Blocking out the memory of her parents death and the sexual violation, somehow made it go away, or at least seem like a bad dream.

All throughout school, Destiny was not very popular. She was extremely quiet and never wanted to draw attention to herself. She didn't have a lot of friends and was usually by herself. She would always read and write mostly love stories, stories of how she envisioned her life to be. Destiny penned these words as she sat in her room, teary eyed and lonely; longing for love:

Will I Ever Know
What Passion, What joy that flows,
Is it real, Can it be real
Will I ever know

It makes me want to live again,
Be free—Experience the rain

It makes me want to laugh and grow—
Be me—be free, but will I ever know
Can it be real, is it real, what joy that flows,
What passion, but will I ever know

She wanted to love and be loved. Simple, she thought, my prince will find me, and we will live happily ever after.

In the stories she wrote, she would be the beautiful princess in distress and a handsome knight on his strong, white horse would come galloping along to rescue her. These were just stories; just her silly little thoughts on paper. These thoughts that floated around in her head daily had gripped her little heart with fear. Thoughts that she created, but knew would never be a reality.

Chapter 2

~ Could This Be It? ~

Those thoughts are what led Destiny to write the poem, <u>Will I Ever Know</u>? Because of the bad things that happened to her, she thought these things would only live in her head; never to truly exist. She wanted the passion, the joy, the love. But was this something she could ever experience? She thought this could never happen to her. Until the day she saw Dwayne—Dwayne Johnson. Everyone called him "D". He was the quarterback for her high school's junior varsity football team. "Oh my!" she thought, "Dwayne Johnson is the coolest guy and sooooo handsome." All the girls were in love with Dwayne. Every day she would see a different girl walking him to class. She wished it could have been her. How she only wished Dwayne would notice her. But with all of the insecurities she carried around, she thought he'd never say a word to her. "I'm not pretty and I'm shaped funny. I'm not a cheerleader or dancer or anything like that. He would never take a second look at me. I don't stand a chance of being with someone like Dwayne," she thought.

Destiny loved to dance. This was something she had done since she was about 11 years old. It was a way of escaping all the pain and confusion she was dealing with. Every afternoon after school she would go to her room, play some of her favorite songs and dance for hours. She was very good, but she didn't think she was good enough. Actually, she never thought she was good enough for anything or anyone. She was very insecure and never believed she could do anything well. Destiny decided it was time to make a change in her life. She wanted something different. She wanted to be different. What a great time to make such a decision! The school was having tryouts for cheerleaders and dancers. Destiny decided that she would try out for the dance team, and to her surprise, she made it! Being a dancer gave her more opportunity to be where Dwayne would be, at least for one class period anyway, and that would be gym. She was such a good dancer that she was chosen as the assistant captain. She thought this was quite an accomplishment. She had done something she never thought was possible. She never thought she was good enough to do something so awesome. Being chosen as assistant captain of the dance team was a real boost for Destiny. She began to have more confidence in herself. She even began to make friends. Eventually, Dwayne began to notice her and they dated. They were the envy of the school. How did this nobody end up as the assistant captain of the dance team and dating the star of the football team?

Dwayne seemed to brighten up Destiny's world. She now had more confidence in herself than she had ever had before. Dwayne gave her such a great feeling of security. She thought she could take on the world as long as he was by her side. They were known around school as D&D. They did everything together. They went everywhere together. He would always tell her how beautiful she was and he always made her feel special—like no one had ever done before. This was the first time that any one, especially a boy, ever paid attention to her. She was so overwhelmed and loved every minute of it. There was nothing he would not do for Destiny. He would pick flowers from the school's Garden Club garden at least twice a week for her. Destiny loved carnations and roses. Dwayne made sure that's what he picked each time. He would get her books from the locker, carry them, and walk her to class. Most of the time he was late for his own class because he wanted to make sure Destiny made it to each class safely. Destiny thought she had found the one. The one that would make all of her dreams come true. The knight on the white horse that she had written about in so many of her stories was Dwayne! She always dreamed that her guy would be handsome, athletic, tall, brave, and very confident. She found all of this in Dwayne. She finally found the love she had so long looked for and desired. She loved Dwayne and there was no reason for her not to show it. He treated her like the princess she had written about in her many stories. He rescued her; and what better way to show her love and appreciation to him than to be intimate with him—or so she thought. He never pressured her, but all of the girls would tell her if she wanted to keep him, she should have sex with him; otherwise, he would find someone else who would. She felt this was the way to keep things as perfect as they were. All she knew was that they were in love—a love that seemed so perfect, so true, so real; a love that was everlasting.

After dating for a year or so, and many sexual encounters, Destiny became pregnant. In Destiny's eyes, this was alright with her. This was just great—better than her favorite vanilla ice cream with hot fudge! This was just simply marvelous because she really loved Dwayne and she knew that he felt the same way about her. She began to think about the painting she saw as a little girl, the picture of the perfect family. She thought she could now have that dream, the perfect family. Despite the fact that the two of them were only in high school, Destiny was sure this was going to work out. She figured they would get jobs and raise the baby together and after graduating from high school, they would get married. She had it all worked out. One windy, but sunny day, as they walked home after school, they stopped in the park where they had stopped so many times before to spend time together before going home. The park was only a few blocks from Destiny's house and a convenient place since they had to pass it on the way home. While Dwayne was pushing her on the swing, Destiny told him that she was pregnant. To her surprise, his response was, "What? Who is it for?" Needless to say, he stopped pushing the swing! "Who have you been with Destiny?" He was seriously angry.

For some strange reason, he thought she had been seeing someone else. Destiny laughed and said "silly, it's yours, it's ours!" Dwayne became silent, so very quiet, so very cold; he then turned away from the swing. He told her he had a lot of homework and chores to do, so it was best he get home. He didn't say anything to her on the remainder of the walk home. She thought it would be best to give it a minute and let it sink in, so she didn't say anything either. He walked Destiny home, kissed her as usual, and told her he'd call her later. Later for Destiny NEVER came. Dwayne never spoke to her again. She tried calling, talking to him at school, waiting for him after practice; she even went to his house a few times, knowing he was there, but he wouldn't come to the door. The kids at school began talking about Destiny. Some of the things she heard were: 'How could she let this happen?' 'What was she thinking?' 'She should have known better.' She would hear this over and over again sounding ever so loudly in her head. "No one is saying anything about him," she thought. "No one is talking about how he's abandoned me and the baby. Everyone is making it sound like I did this all by myself." Full of pain, she continued . . . . "He had a part to play in this also. I can't make a baby by myself." Destiny was truly angry, but still so very much in love with Dwayne. She thought Dwayne could have handled the situation a whole lot better. "Something is so seriously wrong with this picture. No one really cares about how I feel; about what I'm dealing with; or about what I have to go through now." Oh, how she wanted all of this to just go away. This was just the beginning of Destiny's relationship issues.

Chapter 3

~ *Reality Check* ~

*O*ne beautiful spring day, about four years later, as Destiny and Ciara were in the park, Destiny began thinking about her life; what she had and what she wanted; where she was and where she wanted to be. She no longer had to figure life out for herself, but there was Ciara. "She didn't ask to come into this world, but she's here," Destiny thought, "so what do I do now? How do I make a life for the two of us?" Destiny is now in her twenties with a child. She has a job, but it doesn't pay as much as she needs to really live the life she desired for her and Ciara. She has her own place, it's not much; but it's hers. As she sat in the park, she noticed all the couples; they all seemed to be in love. They all seemed so happy. They all seemed so full of joy and contentment. "What about me? What about me?" This was the scream on the inside of her as the tears slowly ran down her cheeks. "How can this happen for me?

Will it ever happen for me?" Ciara's ball rolls across the beautiful thick, green grass towards a gentleman with a little boy. The little boy immediately picks up the ball and throws it to Ciara. As Destiny goes over to check on her, the gentleman introduces himself and apologizes for his son's interference. "No need to apologize," said Destiny, "they're just kids, it's ok." The two of them talk for a few minutes and Destiny returns to her playtime with Ciara. Later that day after putting Ciara to bed, Destiny begins to pray. "Lord, I know we haven't talked much lately, and I know I don't attend church on a regular basis, and when I'm there, I'm really not there, but . . . well . . . um . . . you see . . . . I don't really know how I got to this point in my life." Destiny began to cry and tremble with fear. She reached for a tissue to dry her eyes and took a deep breath. She was truly sorry for her actions or lack of. She continued praying. "I was raised to love you, to serve you and to please you. I always went to church and I even sang in the choir . . . . but somewhere along the way I stopped. I have made so many bad choices in my life. I've been in relationships with people who didn't mean me any good. Some of them used me for sex, while others took my love for granted. Most of them never took me seriously. I never did anything to intentionally hurt anyone, but that was what I received in return . . . . hurt, pain, confusion, questions, doubt, more questions, more doubt, well and the list goes on. God, I have my daughter now, and I want better for her. I want her to have a real life. She should have a life filled with love and joy. I want her to be proud of her momma. So God, I'm just asking for your help . . . . um . . . . AMEN." She slowly walks to the kitchen for a glass of water and stares out the window. She gazes across the street into the night sky. She sees what seemed to be a million and one stars looking back at her. They were so close it looked like she could reach up and touch them. She senses a feeling of peace like she had never felt before. She went to bed and slept the entire night. Not a care in the world. She didn't wake up during the night as she had done so many times before worrying about her life and how she and Ciara would make it. She wakes up the next morning energized and ready to take on the day. She gets Ciara ready for school and she heads off to work.

Chapter 4

~ *The Big Break* ~

*S*he works at one of the largest advertising firms in the city. Destiny is the secretary for the Director of Accounting. Her dream is to one day be in her bosses shoes. She wants to be the Director of an accounting department. She thought if she could get that position, she and Ciara would be financially able to have the life she so desired for them. They would have the best of everything and Ciara could go to the best schools. Destiny is a very hard worker. She's very dedicated and works late whenever the need arises. One day, her boss, Mr. Carroll, tells her there's an opening for a newly created position of Assistant Director of Accounting, and he wants her to apply. Mr. Carroll informs Destiny that he knows she would be great in the position and could someday even become the Director once he retires. That was music to her ears! That was the big break she had been waiting for! She thinks this is great until she read the qualifications for the position. The advertisement read: *Applicants must have a B.S. in Accounting with at least 3 years of experience in the accounting field.* "Another missed opportunity," she thought. "What I thought was an open door has just closed in my face." She only had a high school diploma. After having Ciara at such a young age, she never had an opportunity to further her education. When she graduated high school, she immediately had to get a job to support herself and Ciara. She spoke with Mr. Carroll about the situation and he was willing to work with her to make sure she became the Assistant Director—even though he knew she didn't meet the qualifications. He believed that she could do the job and do it well. Destiny was so excited about her new upcoming position. She thought, "I'm finally on my way!"

That evening, she decides to attend a church a few blocks from her apartment. She and Ciara pulled into the large graveled parking lot. The great big sign read *Greater New Bethel Church*. She could hear the choir singing and the music playing. She was so excited! She and Ciara could not wait to get inside! Ciara was excited as well, because just like her mama, she loved to sing. As Destiny entered the church, she could see the beautiful stained glass windows and the lovely portraits that hung on the walls. There were portraits of a baptismal service, and a communion service. However, the one that really caught her eye was the painting of the families walking to church. The children were carrying bibles in their hands and the ladies wore their wide brim hats. The men were dressed in dark suits, styling hats as well. She could literally see herself being a part of one of those families.

This has been her dream since she saw the painting in the mall.

When the doors were opened to the sanctuary, she saw what looked like hundreds of people standing, clapping, and singing. As she gazed over in the corner of the sanctuary, she saw a man dancing and shouting. Over to the other side of the church she even saw a woman jumping up and down and waving her hands. "Wow!" she thought, "I have never seen anything like this before!" As Destiny and Ciara took their seats they began clapping as well. Before Destiny knew it, she was up on her feet singing right along with the rest of the congregation. She couldn't help it; it was like she was being drawn in by a power stronger and much greater than herself. She felt so happy, so full of joy and excitement. She began reminiscing about when she was a little girl and her aunt would take her to church. She remembered singing in the choir and praising God with everything in her little body. She would clap and sing like there was no tomorrow, she gave it her all whenever she would sing. "This is what's been missing" she said . . . . "God—I've been missing you!"

Destiny and Ciara attended church faithfully every Sunday and for services during the week. After a while, they both joined and became members of Greater New Bethel Church. Destiny, of course, joined the choir. After a few months, she also joined the dance team and became a part of the mission group—working in the kitchen, serving the community and working at the church's shelter. It seems as though her life has some order now. Things seemed to be going great, until one

Wednesday, Mr. Carroll asked her to work late. She had choir rehearsal and didn't want to miss it. She had to choose. She remembered Mr. Carroll wanted her to have the new position as Assistant Director. Trying to desperately please him, she decided to work late instead of attending choir rehearsal. While working late with Mr. Carroll, Destiny rushed into his office, full of energy and enthusiasm. She was eager to show him the quarterly statements she'd prepared that he would need for the departmental meeting first thing in the morning. "Mr. Carroll," she said as she rushed in. "I've completed the statements you requested." "Already,?" he asked. "Go back and check your figures, make sure they are correct." She answered with the utmost confidence, "They are sir. I've checked each section twice and have read the report to make sure I used the correct figures." "Well done, Destiny. You're doing a fantastic job. How about we go out for a bite to eat? It's still early. We can celebrate." "Celebrate what Mr. Carroll?" she asked. "Your promotion girlie, I told you that the job of Assistant Director is yours! Let's just go out. I'll show you a good time. I promise! I'm looking out for you—just want to help you achieve your goals. Think about it, everyone needs a little help from time to time." He starts to walk closer to her. He stops and stares into her eyes and begins to smile. "Wow! You are so beautiful. I have been watching you around here. How your clothes compliment your gorgeous body; how you smell like roses freshly picked from the garden; and when you walk, it seems as though you are floating. Destiny, we can make things happen! We could have something great together. I can definitely make sure you become the Assistant Director. We'll work around that little degree issue—or the lack there of." He gives a little chuckle and turns to walk back to his desk. "Think about my dinner proposal while I straighten things up in here," he said. Destiny returned to her desk. Sitting and thinking and thinking—what's a girl to do? After giving it some thought for a few minutes, which seemed like hours, she decided to go out with him. She wasn't interested in dating him, but she just wanted to amuse him and play along so she could get that job. In Destiny's mind, she was just going to have dinner with her boss—just business—nothing more, nothing less. During dinner, Mr. Carroll made some sexual advances towards Destiny while discussing the job she so desperately wanted. "You know Destiny," said Mr. Carroll, "you wouldn't want to let this great opportunity pass you by." He takes a gulp of his scotch that the waiter had just sat on the table. His other hand now moves under the table and on to Destiny's leg; gently moving it up and down her thigh. She flinches a bit, but doesn't remove his hand. She's feeling uneasy, but this is her boss, she thought. "This night is almost over and I can forget this ever happened" was the thought floating around in her head. As he slowly removed his hand from her thigh he continued on, saying . . . . "You know Destiny, you being the A.D. will put you in a place of financial stability and you would gain the respect of so many in the company. I know that's what you want. We both know you're not making that much money and this promotion is just what you need." They talk about the position a while longer, he has a few more drinks, they finish their dinner and he walks her out of the restaurant. "Thanks for the dinner, sir," said Destiny. "Oh no, thank you, it was my pleasure. You just think about what I said. I can help you get that position. I just need you to continue going out with me from time to time. I love looking at your pretty face and gorgeous bod." He chuckles and walks away to get into his car. As he's getting in his car he yells to her, "See you in the morning and think about what I said!"

After a few 'business dinners' with Mr. Carroll, Destiny feels pressured and sleeps with him because she so desperately wants that job. The sexual relationship continues for several months. She's still going to church, still singing in the choir and dancing at the church services and revivals, still working with the community missions, but she's sleeping with her boss to get a promotion. She is feeling misunderstood and trapped in a situation that she can't seem to find a way out. "What am I to do? What could I do?" These thoughts haunted her day and night. Destiny was unsure. She knew she needed to get out of this situation, but she also wanted that promotion.

Chapter 5

~ Just Another Secret ~

While at choir rehearsal one night, Andre', the choir director, noticed Destiny's glow was disappearing. She didn't seem as excited as she had been before. Destiny was a strong alto and sang lead on several songs. She was just as passionate about singing as she was about dancing. Singing and dancing gave her some type of relief—a way of escape from all the hurt and rejection she had been subjected to. Andre' noticed that she didn't volunteer for lead parts anymore and she wasn't singing the way she used to. Destiny always sang like the Lord himself was standing right before her cheering her on! She had such liberty when she sang. It was as though everything was perfect in a perfect little world, with no hurt, pain, misfortunes, or grief. He knew something was wrong, but didn't know exactly what. He knew Destiny was not the same person she was on the first day he heard her sing. Why was she singing so differently? The passion seemed to have disappeared and the liberty was definitely gone.

One night after rehearsal, he asked her out for a bite to eat. She declined because she had to pick Ciara up from the sitter. She was also a little shy because she thought he was very attractive. Andre' asked Destiny to call him once she'd put Ciara down for bed because there was something he needed to discuss with her. She agreed and called him as he asked. Andre' began the conversation by joking with Destiny about Sister Hattie Mae who was about 60 years old, sang tenor, but always wanted to sing the alto part. As Andre' is still laughing, he questions Destiny. "Ok Destiny, what is really going on with you?" "What do you mean?", she replied. "Something just doesn't seem right. It seems as though something has been distracting you—like something is bothering you." "Man, I have no idea what you're talking about. You must be getting your signals mixed up. Everything is fine; things could not be better!" Destiny laughed it off and began to talk about the new song Andre' had just introduced to the choir. She said she really liked the song, but some parts were a little high for her. He knew she was only avoiding him, so he didn't push the issue. They continued the conversation a few more minutes and then Destiny realized how much time had gone by and that it was really late. "Big day at work tomorrow, Andre'; I really need to make sure I'm alert and ready. I'll have to chat with you later. I've got to get some sleep," she said. She didn't want anyone to know what was going on between her and her boss. She didn't think she could share this with Andre' because she didn't know him that well. She really liked him and didn't want to get him involved in her drama.

As time went on, Andre' and Destiny's relationship as choir member and director eventually grew into something greater. She began to have feelings for Andre', and it was quite evident that he had strong feelings for her as well. This was someone she could see herself with for the rest of her life. Andre' was smart, he loved God, he really cared about Destiny and he made her feel loved, wanted and secure. During their many conversations, Andre' would always tell Destiny how beautiful she was and how lucky he was to have her in his life. She loved the fact that someone really cared for her. Meanwhile she is still in this so-called relationship with her boss. "How do I let this go? This needs to stop, but I want—I mean, I need that promotion," she thought to herself. "I'm trying to make a better life for me and Ciara. I don't have a college degree and this is a great opportunity for me; I can't mess this up." Over and over she rehearses these words in her head. "I can't mess this up." Destiny is sleeping with her boss, Mr. Carroll, for a promotion and she is in a relationship with Andre' for security and approval. "I can't keep lying to myself or to Andre'" she thought. "He deserves better."

A few weeks later, Destiny finds out that Mr. Carroll decided not to fill the position at this time. There would be no Assistant Director of Accounting. Destiny was furious. She stormed into his office to confront him only to hear the words "I've gotten what I wanted; now you can return to your desk or you're fired." As she was slowly walking out of his office, he tells her "hey Destiny, wise up hun. Don't believe everything that someone tells you—everyone is not as honest as you." Yet again, he gives his famous chuckle and tells her to close his door on her way out. Destiny was devastated. She returned to her desk and sat there and cried. She had given the most precious part of herself away to someone she didn't love, who didn't love her and only used her for selfish reasons. She felt so ashamed and guilty at the same time. She thought, "I was using him for a promotion and he was using me for sex. He got what he wanted, but what did I get?—some really bad sex!" She laughed as she wiped her eyes. "Destiny, girl you lose again; right back where you started. Will anything every work out for you—I mean ANYTHING?"

After leaving work, she finds Andre' at the church listening to new songs for the choir. She was so burdened and overwhelmed she needed to talk to someone. She tells Andre' all that has been going on with her job and Mr. Carroll. Andre' couldn't understand why Destiny would do such a thing. He thought she loved herself much more than that. He began to yell at her saying that she was trash and he couldn't believe he fell in love with her. At that very moment, she believed she was no good and could bring no good into Andre's life. So she told Andre' that their relationship was a big lie. She was only using him and she really didn't care for him. "Andre', she said. You were just someone to hang out with." He was furious. They get into this huge argument because Andre' could not believe that the woman he loved would keep such a thing from him, and then tell him that she was only using him; he didn't mean anything to her. He repeatedly asked her why didn't she trust him enough to tell him what had been going on between her and Mr. Carroll? What was wrong with her? What was she thinking? Andre' really came down hard on Destiny, but she had no reply; all she could do was cry. Humiliated and distraught, she finds a room off the side of the sanctuary and cries and cries and cries. She tries to pray, but all that could come out of her mouth was the word 'stupid'. "I'm so stupid" she repeated this over and over and over again. Andre' finds her and tries to apologize for his actions only to get pushed away. "Andre'!", she screams, "I'm no good for you, you deserve better." They get into a yelling match again. Not knowing that Vanessa, the church's walking, talking bulletin board with flashing neon lights, was in the next room. Vanessa over hears the entire conversation. Unknowing to Destiny and Andre', Vanessa tells everyone what went on with Destiny and her boss as well as what was going on with Destiny and Andre'. She told people how they had been secretly seeing each other outside of church activities. This lead to the biggest scandal Greater New Bethel had ever seen. Destiny decides it would be best for everyone if she would leave the church. She knew it would be too much for her to handle. Everyone would be talking about her behind her back and giving her those strange, dirty looks every time she would come to service. She just wasn't strong enough to deal with it. This was only a reminder of how people treated her back in high school when they found out she was pregnant for Dwayne. She just wasn't up to dealing with this all over again.

Chapter 6

~ Finally, I Can Live ~

Several months have passed now, and Destiny has a new job at the same company, but in a different department. She is now attending Rose of Sharon Christian Church and is very content with her life. She takes Ciara to their favorite park one Saturday morning for their usual mother and daughter outing. They spread out Ciara's favorite blanket and decide to lie down. It's a beautiful light blue and yellow blanket with butterflies and clouds. Destiny is reading Ciara's favorite book to her, <u>When The Baby Cries</u> by E. L. Duncan. She hears a voice that says "so we meet again lovely lady." Destiny didn't recognize the voice so she sat up to clearly see who was speaking. It was the gentlemen she'd met in the park some time ago with his son. Tall, handsome, with a beautiful smile; his name was Steve. She invited him and his son to join them as they were about to enjoy their snacks. Destiny had packed Ciara's favorites: peanut butter and jelly sandwiches, bbq potato chips, pickles, and let's not forget the juice—Ciara loved Very Berry Fruity Sunset punch. She would drink this all day if her mom would let her. So the guys joined Destiny and Ciara for snacks. Steve and Destiny talked for hours while the children played. They exchanged phone numbers and soon began dating. Steve was an account executive for the utility company, had been married and divorced, and was 4 years older than Destiny. Steve made Destiny's life great. He treated her like the queen she knew to be deep down inside of her. He took her to the best restaurants, to the theatre, to jazz concerts, to ballets and to art galleries and of course, her favorite, romantic walks in the park. He left no stone unturned. He opened doors for her and pulled her seat out for her to sit. When introducing her to his friends and coworkers, he would always refer to her as his lady, his queen, or his good thing. He gave Destiny the best; the best of everything. Anything Steve thought Destiny wanted or desired and never told him, he would somehow buy it and present it to her in the most romantic ways. Once he bought her a teddy bear and placed a diamond bracelet around its arm. She was so excited she stood there and cried—couldn't say a word! He bought her designer bags and diamond rings, necklaces and watches. He showered her with the finer things, the things she always wanted, but could never afford.

One December night as Destiny was getting dressed to attend Steve's company Christmas party, she began singing and dancing around her bedroom; flashing her diamonds as she practiced greeting the many people who would be in attendance at the party. "Hi I'm Destiny.

It's a pleasure to meet you. Beautiful dress . . ." She looks at the clock and realizes it is well past 8:00pm. "Steve should have been here by now," she said. She calls his phone, but no answer. The clock now says, 9:00pm, then 9:30pm. She calls him again, but still no answer. She decides to drive to his home, but the house was dark and his car was not in the driveway. So she rushes back to her place thinking he'd be there, but he wasn't. It's now 10:45pm. She calls and there is still no answer. She's starting to worry. No Steve. What has happened? She decides to call the nearest hospital to see if anyone fitting his description had been brought in—maybe from a car accident. Nothing . . . there was no one there fitting his description. The clock now says 12:10am. She calls and he finally answers. "Steve!," she says franticly, "are you ok?" "What happened?" He replies in a rather strange and calm voice, "Nothing. Can't talk now, I'll call you later." Destiny is still quite upset, but glad to know he's alive and well. She was relieved that nothing had seriously happened to him. She still had no idea what was going on or what had happened, but settled for knowing he was okay. Destiny had a million and one questions and scenarios in her head as to what could have happened. She finally lies down and falls asleep fully dressed in her beautiful black and silver gown.

She wakes up the next morning and calls him, but gets no answer. She gets ready and goes to work, not able to concentrate on anything. She calls him again, still no answer. She goes to their favorite café for lunch hoping to run into him there, but no luck. No Steve. She waits for what seems like hours for him to arrive, but still no Steve.

She decides to call him from the café, finally, he answers, "yeah hello" in a very dry and unconcerned voice. "Steve, hey it's me Destiny. How are you?" Her voice trembled, as she had no idea what to expect. "Look Dest, I can't talk right now. I'll call you back in about 2 hours," he replied. "Ok hun" she replies, "love you." She hears the dial tone on the other end. Her heart makes this really big thump that seems to fall to the pit of her stomach. She thought that was strange because he never hung up the phone without saying 'I love you my queen' or 'you know I love you girl.' She returns to work still unable to really concentrate, so she takes the rest of the day off. She knows something is wrong, but she can't put her finger on it. She thought, "This is not like Steve at all. I really need to talk to him and find out what's going on." Destiny needed to clear her head and think, so she went to the park where they met. She sat quietly on the bench near the fountain. As she sits on the bench, she sees couples, young and old, holding hands, hugging, kissing, and showing some type of affection. She begins to cry. Something is seriously wrong. "This is not like Steve," she thought. She leaves the park and heads home. Three hours, four hours, now five hours have passed with no call from Steve. She calls him again, he answers "yeah hello," in that same unconcerned voice. "Steve, it's me." "Yeah Dest—I know I was supposed to call you, but I had stuff to do," he says in a dry, stale tone. "Oh, okay, well what's going on? What happened last night? You were supposed to pick me up for the party, but you never came. What happened?," she asked. "Dest look," said Steve, "I can't talk now, I'll call you tomorrow." Well,

Destiny waited and waited. Steve never called her again. She had no idea what happened, why he didn't call, why he left her, why he abandoned her. What did she do? All of these questions, but no answers.

Chapter 7

~ Woman To Woman ~

*D*estiny was so distraught she had to take some time off from work to pull herself together. She still tried calling Steve, but decided to eventually give up since he would not answer any of her calls. Anita, one of Destiny's coworkers, calls her to see why she hadn't been at work for the past few days. Anita was about the same age as Destiny and had been married and divorced twice. Anita now felt that men were users and she wanted no part of that any more. Her first husband, Terrance, was a repairman and almost everyday he would come home smelling like some woman's cheap perfume. He would never take her out because he always had to fix some needy woman's sink or toilet. He never had time to spend with Anita, including time for intimacy or sex. Their marriage was short lived. They soon divorced, and she met Chris. Chris was the general manager at the local grocery store. He always had time for her and they had mad sexual encounters—all the time! . . . . The problem with this relationship was that he was an 'in the closet' alcoholic. He hid it well—at least until the day Anita asked him to use the car to go get her hair done. Something set him off and he began hitting her like she was a man. He pinned her against the wall and choked her until she almost passed out. He left her that day and she has not heard from him since. Later, she found bottles of alcohol throughout the house. From those experiences, Anita closed her heart to men. She started focusing her attention to females because they are in no way like men. They are sensitive and concerned about their partner. Men sometimes brush women off and don't think it bothers them. Men use women for sex and money and when they've gotten enough or they've gotten what they wanted, they leave them. Women understand each other and a woman would never treat her like the men from her past. This was simply Anita's point of view.

Anita decided to call Destiny. She told her that she was worried because she had not seen her at work for a few days. Destiny briefly fills her in on some of the situation and invites her over so they can continue talking. Destiny was really lonely and needed a shoulder to cry on. They talked about Destiny's situation for a while and Anita assured her that she would be there for her through all of this. "Dest, I know this is hard, but I got you girl," Anita said, as she renders a soft and gentle smile. She continues to comfort Destiny; then gets up from the couch to pour Destiny a glass of her favorite red wine while listening to more of her horrible story about Steve. She even tells her about her past relationship with Andre' and how she loved him or thought she did, but it didn't work out between the two of them because she didn't trust him enough to be honest with him. She began thinking that maybe she wasn't honest with Andre' because she was afraid he would abandon her like so many others. She thought about how her parents abandoned her, Dwayne, and now Steve; she couldn't bare another person leaving her; shutting her out of their life.

Anita began to share with Destiny how her marriages were nothing but lies. How Terrence and Chris never really loved her, and how she gave everything in both of the relationships. She told her how both of her ex-husbands only used her as a security blanket. They knew she would be there to hold everything down; to keep things together—and she was. She did exactly that. Destiny begins to talk about Steve again. "Oh how I miss him," she said, crying uncontrollably, as if she just found out her best friend had died. Anita began to console Destiny with soft touches, hugs, and a stroke of the hair from her face. She wiped the tears from her eyes and passionately held her. Destiny knew within herself that something didn't feel right about the hug or the soft touches, but she needed to be held right then. Anita told her how she could treat her better than Steve ever did. She told her how she deserved better and she was her better. They continued their conversation a while then Anita arose from the couch to leave. She kissed Destiny softly on the cheek as she gave her a hug, and another kiss. "I love you Destiny," Anita said, "I always have. Let me be there for you." Destiny replied, "Thanks Nita, good night, we'll talk later."

After Anita left, Destiny began to think about all the things Anita shared with her about men. "From my point of view," said Destiny, "all men are dogs. They can't be trusted. They use you to get what they want then they leave you with no explanation. They hurt you and don't even care. Why do I keep putting myself through this? One bad relationship after another," she thought. "Maybe I should give Anita a try, or at least just hang out with her and see what happens." Time goes on and Anita and Destiny hang out even more. They really enjoy each other's company. They began spending countless hours together. They'd go out to dinner and the movies. They even took Ciara to the amusement park every other weekend. On a few occasions Destiny would enjoy those long sensual foot rubs Anita would give her after a long day. But Destiny knew that this was not right. She was starting to think about Anita during the day. She was even having sexual thoughts about her. "Dest, girl, catch yourself," she said. Destiny knew she was not raised this way. She was having feelings for another woman. God did not intend a relationship of this nature to be between two women. God's plan is for a man and a woman to marry, be in an intimate relationship together, have children and live happily ever after. She's got to let Anita know this relationship can never be more than a friendship. Destiny questions herself within. "When will I ever find love, true love? Will I ever know what true love feels like? What's wrong with me that I can't ever love someone and they love me right back?"

Destiny decided to curl up on the couch and read one of her favorite books. It was a book of poetry by

Tomia Lee. One of Destiny's favorite poems to read was entitled *Me*. She sat thinking about all of the relationship problems she had encountered and where her life was headed. She reaches over to the table next to her for a glass of wine. She sips, returns the glass to the table and begins to read.

I am who I am but who am I

Am I the little rich girl or am I just plain Jane

Am I the little angel as I'd like to proclaim

Am I who I am or am I who I want to be

Really someone please tell me

I am ME whoever that is

Confused abused and misused

I am ME

No test no quiz no joke man this is for real

Full of hurt pain over and over again

Whoever I am whatever state I'm in

Simply put

I am ME

She continues reading from her book of poetry and falls asleep with the book in her lap.

Chapter 8

~ Strictly Platonic ~

*J*ust as she's questioning her relationship with Anita, Jason gives her a call. Jason is another coworker. He thought the world of Destiny, and always found time for her. Regardless of what was going on in his life, if she needed him, he was there. She found him to be a true friend. There was a time when Destiny's car broke down on the weekend and she had no one to call for help. She remembered Jason told her if she ever needed anything to give him a call. So she did. Jason immediately stopped what he was doing and ran to her rescue. He was at his family's bar-b-cue, but leaving was no big deal to him. Destiny was much more important to him than anyone else; than anything else. He managed to fix her car enough to get it to the shop to be repaired. Jason was such a great guy; he even paid the mechanic for repairing the car and would not accept repayment from Destiny. There was another time when Destiny was out of food for her house and she had no idea what she and Ciara would eat. They were down to the last few slices of bread, the last bottle of soda, and the last pack of meat. Again, Jason helps out by taking her to the store and buying grocery for her and Ciara. He really liked Ciara and thought of her as his own. She called him Uncle J. He really liked that! Jason had never been married, and he had no children, so he had nothing but time for Destiny and Ciara. Jason was a really nice guy; a really good guy, but he wasn't just being nice to Destiny for no reason. He truly loved her. Jason loved her from the moment he laid eyes on her. They had been friends since she started with the company. He remembered that day so well. He was walking down the hall taking some files to the file room and stepping off the elevator were these long luscious legs. She stepped off the elevator and headed to the receptionist desk. As she walked, it seemed as though she was walking on air. Her long curly hair bouncing as she glided so graciously to the desk. Oh and the voice; speaking ever so calmly and serene. "Hi. I'm looking for the Human Resource Department." This vision seemed to be an angel, gently floating her way into his life. Jason wanted so badly to ask Destiny to have lunch with him and some of the other coworkers, but he would always be so nervous. Just the thought of being in her presence sent feelings through him like none he'd ever felt before. He wondered if he would ever be able to get this vision of loveliness to somehow talk to him. One day as they arrived to work around the same time, Jason was able to hold the door open for Destiny as she entered the building. "Good Morning," he said with a smile as bright as the sun. "Good morning; thank you," she replied and smiled right back at him. Every day after that, Jason would make it a point to be somewhere, anywhere he thought Destiny would be. They soon began to have short conversations in passing. They would occasionally have lunch together and sometimes would stop by each other's office for a short chat. This grew into such a great friendship. But, Jason had fallen in love with Destiny. He wanted more.

Jason decided to call and check on Destiny because he had not seen her in the office for a few days. They decided to meet up for dinner that evening. They met at the local sports bar for a small dinner and drinks. Destiny ordered their famous chicken fingers and fries and Jason ordered a pizza with everything on it. They sat, ate, and chatted for a while. He knew just what to say to see her beautiful smile. He always knew how to make her laugh. He was so charming, and she loved the attention. Then came the big question; Jason wanted to know if what he had been seeing was real. He told Destiny how he had noticed her and Anita together more than usual. He told her how he had seen Anita touching her and brushing her hair from her face one day as they sat out in the courtyard on their break; and that just didn't seem right to him. He told her that one day he noticed them arguing, and then he saw Anita pull her close and hug her. He also saw how they would go off to the balcony at work to eat instead of eating in the dining area with everyone else. Destiny told him of their relationship and that she decided to end it. She hadn't told Anita yet, but she was going to. Jason once again let Destiny know that he would always be there for her for whatever she needed, and he meant that—whatever she needed. He gently reached across the table to hold her hand; she gave a big sigh and slowly pulled her hand back. "J" she said, "I know you've always been there for me, but . . . . I can't do this now. I'm so confused; I don't know what to do. I don't know what I want." "It's ok," he replied. "Like I said, I'll always be here for you." She smiled and said "thanks love, I know you will. You are a real good friend, a true friend." They finished their meal and ended the evening at Spanky's, which was a dance club across the street from the sports bar. They had a blast. Destiny really felt at ease with "J". She could be herself and enjoy the moment; not worrying if anyone was giving her strange looks or talking about her. When she was with "J" nothing or no one else mattered. She truly trusted him and enjoyed his company. Oh yeah, and the boy could dance too! Even though she was enjoying the night, it was a bit awkward for Destiny because she really liked "J" and didn't want to hurt him. She loved him, but she wasn't in love with him. It was quite clear to her that he felt differently towards her. She realized that "J" was really in love with her. He was the only man that has ever been in her life who seemed to genuinely care about her, but there was something missing. Even though he respected her and never pressured her for sex, she couldn't figure out why she didn't love him differently. They enjoyed a night together full of laughter and good ole fashioned fun. Their night ended with a friendly hug and kiss and they went their separate ways.

Chapter 9

~ It's All Over, Or Is It? ~

*I*t's been approximately one year since the horrible break up with Steve. For some reason Destiny just can't get him out of her mind. She still remembers all the dreams and plans they shared. She desperately wants Steve back, but realizes he is out of her life for good. This devastation and tragic event has caused her to become withdrawn and alone. She now missed work on a regular basis. She didn't take Ciara to the park anymore, and she even stopped going out after work with the gang. This has been a bit much for her, but she handles it gracefully. Whenever she's at work, she pretends that she is living the best of life. She brags (lies) about all the fun she's having with friends that are not associates of her work friends. She talks about the many different guys she's dating, and there's usually a weekend trip or two she would throw in the conversation. Destiny is realizing her life is over. Without Steve and those magical dreams they shared, she had nothing but one lie after another.

One brisk October evening, she asked Marcel, her next door neighbor, to watch Ciara for a few hours until she ran an errand. To Marcel, this usually meant she'd met a new man and was going out to dinner or something along those lines. This was not unusual because she and Marcel would watch each other's children from time to time. Destiny decided to drive out to Lake Shawnee where she and Steve spent a lot of their evenings. They would go there and talk and have picnics by candlelight. She began reminiscing about all of the wonderful times they shared. She particularly remembered the night they decided to go skinny dipping in the lake. She was so scared because she'd never done anything like that before. But for some reason, when she was with Steve, nothing was impossible for her. She felt like Wonder Woman and she imagined him as Superman. Together they were great—unstoppable even! That evening, they skinny dipped in the lake and made love for what seemed like hours. Well, until the police officer, Officer P. Dilly, decided to ruin their evening by giving them both citations for indecent exposure. She was so embarrassed. But as usual, Steve made everything okay. They began laughing about the entire situation. Then he held her close; well after they put their clothes on! He held her close and spoke softly into her ear, telling her how much he loved her and how beautiful the water looked on her caramel skin, glowing and glistening in the moonlight. Just the thought of that night made her smile, then she began laughing, then she began to cry. Again, she realized that all of that was over. This was just great memories of a wonderful time in her life. She wanted more; she still wanted Steve back. She wanted that part of her life back again.

As she sat in her car with the windows down, gazing into the sky, she began to ask herself what went wrong. What was it that she'd done to drive such a wonderful man out of her life? She began crying and shaking uncontrollably. She opened the glove box to search for a tissue. While searching the glove box she found a screwdriver. Without even thinking, she picked up the screwdriver and began pushing it into her arm, harder and harder. It was as though someone else was doing this to her. She pushed it up and down, from her wrist to her elbow. Again and again, still crying and shaking, she pushed it harder and again from her wrist to her elbow. Pain, she felt none. It was as though she was numb. She began bleeding, then realized how badly she had harmed herself. She dropped the screwdriver and immediately stopped crying. She screamed "STOP IT!, WHAT IS WRONG WITH YOU? WHAT ARE YOU DOING?" Destiny realized at that moment she really needed someone to talk to. She desperately needed help. She thought about calling "J ", but she didn't want to get him upset with her. "I have no one," she thought. She calmed herself down and wrapped an old shirt that she found in the back of the car around her arm to slow down the bleeding. She drove home and immediately ran to Marcel for help. She knocks on the door hard enough for Marcel to hear, but not as hard as she wanted to—too afraid of disturbing the neighbors. Marcel opens the door and immediately asked what happened. Just as Destiny thought, the kids were asleep. Marcel and Destiny quietly stepped into the bathroom to check the damage done to her arm. She could not believe what she had done; all the damage she'd caused to herself. Thankfully, Marcel had recently received her nursing degree and was working at the local clinic. Marcel was able to clean and stitch Destiny's arm. It wasn't as bad as it appeared when she first walked in the apartment. After explaining everything to Marcel, Destiny realized she could have taken her own life and all over someone who didn't give a penny or a nickel about her. This man did not want her anymore. He wasn't even man enough to tell her why he ended the relationship. At that point, it was no doubt in her mind she had better get it together. She had a daughter to look after and a life to live. It may not have been the great life she wanted, but it was hers.

Chapter 10

~ When Sunday Comes ~

*S*unday morning comes and Destiny finds her way back to church. This time, she goes to Greater New Bethel. Not receiving a warm welcome, she enters the sanctuary anyway. Nervous and unsure of what to expect, but she knew how she felt when she was at New Bethel. It was like God himself was sitting next to her expressing his love towards her. Every song sung, every message preached, it was like God was talking directly to her; encouraging, lifting, strengthening, approving and blessing her. As she sat during the service, her mind wandered back to when she was sexually abused. She thought, "How could someone do that to a little girl? I was only 10 years old. What had I done? I didn't bother him. I never said anything to him. Why? What did I do to make him do this to me?" She thought about Dwayne and how he abandoned her and Ciara. "Why did Dwayne leave me? I thought we were in love. I thought he loved me. He never said a word to me after I told him I was pregnant—pregnant with his child. He's never even seen Ciara. He's never even once called to ask about her. What did I do that was so wrong? I think we both made the decision to have sex together. I didn't do this by myself, yet I feel I'm the only one that is being punished. I thought he wanted to be with me as much as I wanted to be with him." She thought about all the men she slept with trying to find love, to be loved, to be noticed, to be accepted. She thought about Mr. Carroll, how he used her for his selfish reasons. He only wanted her for sex, nothing more, and nothing less. "I was just a toy to him. I was just something for him to pass the time. He was never interested in me as a person." She thought about Steve, oh how she loved Steve. She thought about how he left her and even till this day, she still doesn't know why. She was good to him. He was good to her. They did everything together. "He seemed to be so happy with me. We were good together. He could always make me laugh, especially when he did that cute little thing with his lips! What did I do? Why do men keep leaving me?," she thought. "We made plans to get married. We looked at several neighborhoods we wanted to live once we were married. We were making plans to be together for life. What happened?" She thought about how she almost fell into a relationship with Anita only to feel accepted, hoping not to get hurt again. She figured she'd try a relationship with a woman since the men from her past had wronged her. She found everything in Anita that she was looking for, and Anita loved her, she took care of her. It wasn't about sex; it was about security, acceptance, and being appreciated. Anita loved her just the way she was. Emotions ran high, tears streamed down her face. Her heartbeat began to accelerate. Her palms began to sweat. Her point of view . . . "No man can ever love me the way I need to be loved. No man can ever understand me being sexually abused. They will think I asked for it. They will think I did something to entice or provoke him. But that was not the case. I was just walking to the store; I was just a little girl." The tears still falling . . . . "No man will ever know what I felt when I thought I had to sleep with my boss to get promoted. No man will ever understand my struggles. No man will ever accept me for who I am. I'm damaged goods. No man will ever understand how I harmed myself and didn't think my life was worth living because a man dumped me. No man will ever want me now . . . . Who will ever understand?"

She's thinking of all this as the minister is telling the congregation about the love of God, and how we must first love ourselves and respect ourselves if we want others to love and respect us. He's encouraging the people not to give up on life. Just because bad things have happened to you, don't give up. Keep pressing forward. It's all in God's plan. He has a plan for your life, but you've got to hang in there to the end. Destiny realized at that point, she was looking for love and acceptance in all the wrong places. What she so desperately needed to do was to accept herself, love herself, and accept God and his love for her, with or without a man . . . . It was just that simple! Destiny dried her eyes, lifted her head and sat straight up on the pew. She began to say "God loves me . . . . God loves me . . . . And I love me too." Oh the joy she felt saying and hearing those words! She continued saying, "God loves me! God loves me!" This was something she found to be true. God did love her, and she realized she needed to love herself. None of those things that happened was her fault, and none of it meant that God didn't love her. None of it meant that she wasn't a good person. She may have made some bad choices, but it never stopped God from loving her. She now had to accept the choices she'd made and simply move on with life and with God.

After that day Destiny's life was never the same. She understood true love. You love because you choose to. If you feel you have to, then it's not really love. Love is a choice. None of those men she encountered 'chose' to truly love her. They may have cared about her for their own selfish reasons, but none of them really loved her, and she realized maybe she didn't really love them either. "What is important is that Jesus made a choice to love me," she thought. "It had nothing to do with what I had done or where I lived, who I knew, what I knew, or what kind of education I had. He loves me unconditionally. None of those guys cared about me; who I was or what I wanted. Most of them never took the time to get to know me." She left Greater New Bethel that day a changed woman. She no longer cared about what people thought of her. All she knew was that she was loved by God, her creator, and that was enough for her!

Chapter 11

~ When You Least Expect It ~

*D*estiny continued attending Greater New Bethel. She joined the choir and dance team again. She also returned to assisting the community missions group. These were things that Destiny loved and believed had to be a part of her life; a duty and service to God. She was rendering to him all of her that she could. She found something at Greater New Bethel that she knew had to be a part of her everyday living. Her life took a turn for the better. Destiny had now been catapulted in so many areas of her life. She was more focused than ever. She could see clearer than she'd ever seen before.

A few years later, Destiny received a promotion on her job to Budget Analyst for the Executive Budgeting Department. In this position she supervised an entire section of Analyst, which consisted of approximately ten people. She was considered to be the second in charge of the Budgeting Department. She then purchased her first home! Destiny was able to afford a place she and Ciara could finally call home. It was a 4 bedroom, 2 and a half bath house. The flooring throughout the home was dark, natural wood. The most up-to-date appliances in the kitchen, and she was able to fully furnish it with beautiful new furniture. Some of the things she's always wanted and thought she could never afford. She was also able to purchase a new car. She thought life couldn't get any better. This was it! She didn't need a man to be fulfilled or complete. She was completely whole and satisfied knowing that God loved her and she began loving herself. Loving herself was the hardest thing for her to do because she blamed herself for everything that went wrong in her life—in her relationships. She had always looked for a man to complete and to approve her. She realized that was God's job, and He was very good at it!

She was truly content with the life she was living. She was in a place that nothing else mattered to her but loving God and taking care of Ciara. As long as she loved God and lived a life pleasing to him, she knew He had her back. She no longer was in search of love. She'd found it in and through Jesus Christ! She knew He loved her unconditionally, and most importantly, she began loving herself. He would never leave her like all of those guys did. He would always be there for her, to talk to or to just listen. Her job situation was great. She was able to move to another department and show off how smart she really was with no strings attached. She didn't have to sleep with anyone to get the job or keep it. She earned the position by working hard and being faithful to the company. She didn't need a man to pay her bills or to take her out to dinner. God had been her provider all along, she just didn't realize it. She didn't need a man to tell her how beautiful she was or how much he loved spending time with her. God had already told her these things; she just had to believe it. She felt like she could shout from the roof top—"Life is great! It couldn't get any better than this!"

While at the church practicing before dance rehearsal, a gentleman walks in and introduces himself as Micah DeVaul and asks for the Pastor. She shows him to the secretary's office and returns to her practice. Mr. DeVaul was an Evangelist from a nearby city who was going to be speaking at Greater New Bethel for their upcoming revival. After a brief meeting, the pastor and Mr. DeVaul returned to the sanctuary where Destiny was practicing. The pastor introduced Destiny and Mr. DeVaul and told him that she was one of their lead dancers and would probably dance the night he was to speak. Mr. DeVaul couldn't help but notice how beautiful Destiny was; and trying not to stare, he looked away for a few seconds then smiled at her and said, "can't wait to see you dance, looks like you're pretty good." Destiny softly replied, "thank you sir," and returned the smile. As the pastor walked Mr. DeVaul to the door, he asked him to come to his home for dinner that night. There would be a few people from the church there and it would be a good time for them to get acquainted before the revival. "Sounds lovely," Mr. DeVaul said, and graciously accepted the pastor's invitation to dinner.

That night at dinner, there were about 8 members from the church including Destiny. Mr. DeVaul got a chance to speak with all of the members, but it was something special about Destiny. Everyone had an opportunity to tell a little about themselves and Mr. DeVaul was really impressed with Destiny's story. She told him how her parents died when she was a little girl, and how she had a beautiful daughter named Ciara. She didn't go into detail about her personal life, but Mr. DeVaul could see there was much more to Destiny and that she had been through much, and overcame much as well. She told him how she loved to dance and sing for the Lord.

Mr. DeVaul was about 5'7", had a head of curly, black hair with a few hints of grey, thin mustache and a nicely trimmed beard; and was what some women would call sophisticated and attractive. He had no bulging muscles or the infamous six-pack that all the young ladies love to see on their men. However, he did have gorgeous eyes, a great smile, magnificent personality and a wonderful sense of humor.

While speaking with Mr. DeVaul at dinner, Destiny found him to be a very humble, kind, and intelligent man. He loved God and didn't care who knew it. When he spoke of different experiences with the Lord, he was very sincere and passionate. He thanked God for everything that happened in his life—good or bad. She had never met anyone like that before. He was so open about his relationship with the Lord; full of excitement as he captured everyone with his many testimonies of witnessing and sinners giving their lives to the Lord. He told many testimonies of the deliverance of prostitutes and drug users, gang bangers and drug dealers. He shared stories of children growing up in bad homes and abused, but God delivered them from the situations they were in. Destiny could have listened to him speak all night. She found him to be very interesting and genuine. This was something she was not accustomed to—honesty and sincerity.

Mr. DeVaul spoke at the revival the very next week. Everyone talked about how well he ministered. His message was about getting back to the basics. He said that sometimes in our walk with the Lord, because of the day to day things we deal with, we sometimes lose focus of what's important. He stressed how important it is for the people of God to return to the basics of their relationship foundation with Christ; repentance, prayer, worshipping God in spirit and truth, and telling others about the love of Christ. The people really believed he was sincere with his words. They could sense the presence of God as he was ministering, as if God himself was speaking. Mr. DeVaul would attend Greater New Bethel whenever he was in town; which was often, and would minister an awesome word each time he was given the opportunity. His messages changed the lives of many of the people forever.

A few months past and Mr. DeVaul moved to the city a few miles from the church and became a member of Greater New Bethel. He and Destiny worked closely with the Missions Ministry and would oversee many of the revivals for the church. They even spear headed the church's first annual youth retreat as well as organized the street ministering team at the church. Mr. Devaul would minister to the young men and Destiny would minister to the young ladies. Now you're probably wondering, what did she possibly have to offer those young girls after all she'd done and been through? Well, she asked God the same thing! Her life had now become her ministry! Her tests had become her testimonies! Her trials were now her victories!

She and Mr. DeVaul became closer and began to date. They began to share stories of their past, and they saw how much they had in common. They related to each other very well and would talk for hours about everything. Destiny wondered—what could this man possibly see in a woman like her. "This is probably going to end up like all the rest," she thought. But there was something different that made her think again. He didn't treat her like Dwayne and not address issues. He believed that communication was extremely important in relationships. Not just communication, but EFFECTIVE COMMUNICATION. He explained to her that in relationships, the line of communication must always be open, and all parties involved should be on the same page, in the same book. She had never heard of anything like this before—where did this man come from??? "No secrets, no hidden agendas," he said. He didn't treat her like Steve and give her the best of everything. He never bought her diamonds or pearls, clothes or shoes, but he did treat her like a queen, with love and respect. He gave of himself and always did his best to ensure she was happy. He didn't have a big bank account, but he did have *a great big God!*—the God who made the universe and everything in it. He loved her enough to pray with her and for her. He would always make sure that whatever he could do to show Destiny his love for her, he did it.

He loved her and she loved him right back. She fell in love with his spirit, the real him. She fell in love with his character and the fact that he was a man of integrity. He was humble, yet bold. He was gentle, yet stern. She fell in love with him because he walked the walk and talked the talk. He never said what he wanted to do or be. He simply was it and did it. She realized that every guy she's been in a relationship with never measured up to her true desire of a man. But Micah did. He wasn't perfect, but he was perfect for her.

She had a man who looked past all of her insecurities and taught her how to trust God, people, and the God in her. He taught her how to let the past be the past so she could embrace her present and enjoy her future. Of course, this was not an easy thing for Destiny to do. Always lingering in the back of her mind was the fact that no one has ever truly loved her. Lingering in the back of her mind, was the fact that none of her other relationships ever worked out, so why would this one be any different? She couldn't help but to wonder why. Why was it that Dwayne abandoned her; not only her, but Ciara as well. She couldn't help but wonder what caused Steve to just walk away with no explanation. Did she come on too needy? Was she not needy enough? What was it that pushed Steve away? He left with no explanation and this chapter in her life was not closed. She really needed to know why men would come and go in and out of her life so easily. After praying about the situation regarding Steve, she understood that it didn't matter why he left. The most important thing was that she forgave him for leaving without explanation and she could now go on with God and live a productive life. Why does Micah accept her for who she is, for what she is and for what she is not? Why is Micah still around? What's so different about him? He loved her just the way she was; scars, bruises, hurts and insecurities. Somehow he was able to get through to her like no one else could. She then understood what he meant when he explained that by holding on to her past hurts and issues, she could never fully embrace what was in front of her. The true love she'd desired from childhood; her knight on the white horse, the man to rescue her was now in her life. The best thing about it was that he wanted to be there. He wasn't asking or looking for anything in return except for her to love him back. They both wanted to give love and be loved. He may not look as she pictured in all of her stories, and he didn't come galloping into her life on a white horse, but he was there, loving her just for her. This is the man she'd desired all of her life; a man who truly loved God because he would know how to love her. Not showing love by buying her expensive things, or taking her to fancy restaurants, but by loving her from the inside out.

Their relationship blossomed into something beautiful. Ciara began to love and respect Micah because she could see that he really did love her mother and her as well. They would go on outings and have picnics in the park together. They would attend church together regularly. Micah would spend time reading to Ciara and teaching her how to play the piano. There was so much love within this triangle.

One day, Micah decided to meet Destiny for lunch. He knew how much she loved the park, so that's where they met. The sun was shining, but not too bright; the wind was blowing lightly, and there was the smell of popcorn and hot links lingering in the area from the nearby vendors. Destiny and Micah embrace as he gives her a soft and delicate kiss. They sit on the park bench and began talking. After a few minutes of chit-chat, Micah's decides to get up from the bench and kneel beside Destiny. "Destiny, hun," he said, "I know we haven't dated for a long time, I mean years and all, but it seems like I've known you all my life. I must tell you that you are definitely everything I want and need in a wife." "Wife?" asked Destiny. As she's speaking, a man comes over and hands her a single red rose, and begins to play softly on the violin. "Yes, Destiny, wife, my wife for life . . . . Will you marry me?" Nervousness, excitement, and fear, are all the emotions flowing through her at this moment. "Mar . . . Mar . . . Marry you?" she asked. "Oh Micah, are you sure you want to marry me?" "Yes in deed girl!, you are the sunshine in my life, the one who makes my days brighter, and my nights warmer . . . . Yes, Destiny, I want to marry you—will you marry me?" he asked again. "Yes, Micah—Yes! Yes! I will marry you!" she replied, with excitement and joy.

Needless to say, she took the rest of the afternoon off and spent it with Micah. They couldn't wait to pick Ciara up from school to tell her the good news. She was so excited when they told her because she really liked Micah. Ciara now felt as though she could have a mom and a dad. Destiny now felt as though her life was at the place she had dreamed of for so long, and Micah knew he'd found his rib!

Long engagement, no way! They decided to get married 3 months later at Ciara and Destiny's favorite spot. Yes sir, the park! There was a beautiful gazebo with lots of roses: pink, yellow, white and red. There was also a small waterfall near the gazebo. They decided to have a small wedding with family and a few close friends. They became one big happy family! Micah was later ordained as the Assistant Pastor at Greater New Bethel and Destiny continued dancing and singing. They continued working together with the youth and the missions. Micah and Destiny eventually became overseers of several crusades going from town to town ministering to hundreds of souls giving them invitation after invitation to give their lives to Christ.

Life was wonderful, God was blessing, and dream after dream came true for the DeVauls. Sure, they had their share of misunderstandings and problems, as wellw as ups and downs just as any couple would, but they chose to place God in the center of their relationship. Destiny didn't know life with God could be so good. Pleasing God with her life is all she'd ever wanted to do. Sure, she made mistakes, made some bad choices, but God never left her. He was only waiting for her to realize how much she needed Him, and how much He loved her. She knew it in her head, but her heart was saying there was more she had to do to find the love she wanted. Man after man, disappointment after disappointment, heartache after heartache, this is all she found while trying to find love.

There are many counterfeits out there, and yes, she had her share of them. But now things were definitely different for her. It wasn't because she had **a man**; it was because she allowed God to shape her into the woman He saw from the beginning. Sure, she went through a lot. Most of it brought on by the bad choices she made. It may not have seemed like it at the time, but that was how she grew. Sometimes we have to experience **the no,** so we can appreciate **the yes**. He placed the **right man for her**, in the right place at the right time. Wait on God. His desire is that we live as Adam and Eve in the Garden of Eden in the beginning; living on top, blessed, healthy, wealthy, and prosperous. Oh, and while you're waiting, learn to live, love, laugh and enjoy life with God.

. . . . and this is from a woman's point of view!

Conclusion

*S*o, we have visited for a brief moment, the life of Destiny. If you find yourself living as Destiny lived, remember that God is able. Oh yes, God is able! He is no respector of persons. That means, if He took the time to show Destiny His love and power and to bring her to an expected end, He can do the same thing for you!

If you're confused, misused, or abused, you are in the right place for your miracle. You're in the right place for your blessing. Let go of your thoughts, desires and ideas and find out what God has for you—find out what God is saying to you.

Just like Destiny, we all have tried it our way; only to find out is was the wrong way. As Destiny yielded herself to God and realized how much He loved her, she opened the door for the blessings of God to run her down and overtake her! Don't let your past determine your future, but let it propel you into your future . . . . into your DESTINY!

As young girls, we all have dreams of becoming successful in life, whether it is becoming a doctor, a lawyer, a teacher, a mother, or a wife. Whatever path we choose, we want to be successful.

Success is a journey. Every choice, every decision and every action is a determining factor to your destination. Don't expect overnight success. Be determined to work hard for what you want. Be determined to study the Word of God. Be determined to live holy. Be determined to live as God has instructed. Be determined and . . . . Enjoy the journey!

Some of What's Inside!

It's Okay to be Different Setting Boundaries
You Don't Owe Him Anything   Knowing Who You Are

Available at www.xulonpress.com

OR

Email: Mz. Yvette at agirlsguide23@yahoo.com

Contact Information

We hope that you have enjoyed this book by Mz. Yvette. If you would like to contact the author for a speaking engagement or to order books please send emails to: agirlsguide23@yahoo.com